The Legal Framework of
Police Powers

T0383629

Titles in the Legal Framework Series

The Legal Framework of the Constitution
Leonard Jason-Lloyd

The Framework of Criminal Law
Leonard Jason-Lloyd

The Framework of the English Legal System
Leonard Jason-Lloyd

The Legal Framework of the European Union
Leonard Jason-Lloyd and Sukhwinder Bajwa

The Legal Framework of the Modern Company
Leonard Jason-Lloyd and Larry Mead

The Legal Framework of Police Powers
Leonard Jason-Lloyd

The Legal Framework of

Police Powers

Leonard Jason-Lloyd

*Lecturer in Law, University of Derby and visiting Lecturer in
Law at the Midlands Centre for Criminology and Criminal Justice at
Loughborough University, and the Scarman Centre for the Study of
Public Order at the University of Leicester*

FRANK CASS
LONDON • PORTLAND, OR.

Published in 1997 in Great Britain by
FRANK CASS & CO. LTD.
Newbury House, 900 Eastern Avenue,
London IG2 7HH, England

and in the United States of America by
FRANK CASS
c/o ISBS
5804 N.E. Hassalo Street
Portland, Oregon 97213-3644

Copyright © Frank Cass & Co. Ltd. 1997

British Library Cataloguing in Publication Data

Jason-Lloyd, Leonard
    The legal framework of police powers
    1. Police power – England
    I. Title II. Police powers
    344.2'02418

                    ISBN 0 7146 4775 6 (cloth)
                    ISBN 0 7146 4286 X (paper)
                    ISSN 0965-3473

Library of Congress Cataloging-in-Publication Data

Jason-Lloyd, Leonard, 1945-
    The legal framework of police powers / Leonard Jason-Lloyd.
        p.   cm. – (The legal framework series)
    Includes bibliographical references and index.
    ISBN 0-7146 4775 6 (cloth) ISBN 0-7146-4286-X (paper)
    1. Police–Great Britain. 2. Arrest–Great Britain. 3. Searches
and seizures–Great Britain. 4. Detention of persons–Great
Britain. I. Title. II. Series.
KD4839.J37   1996
345.41'052–dc20
[344.10552]   96-26294
                                                              CIP

*All rights reserved. No part of this publication may be reproduced in any form or
by any means, electronic, mechanical, photocopying, recording or otherwise,
without the prior permission of Frank Cass and Company Limited.*

Printed in Great Britain by
Cromwell Press Ltd., Melksham, Wilts.

I dedicate this book to all those in the
police service who constitute
the thin blue line
and especially to those in WD and VW Divisions
who for several years were my colleagues.

Contents

Preface

General interest in the study of police powers has increased substantially in modern times, particularly since the early 1980s when it became evident through a spate of serious disorder that more of the public were beginning to question police authority. In response to pressure from a number of sources in addition to general public concern, the Police and Criminal Evidence Act 1984 was passed which constituted possibly the single greatest reform of police powers this century. It is this statute which will receive the focus of attention of this book, although not to the exclusion of all else. Since 1984 Parliament has intervened further by enacting a number of additions to police powers including, more recently, the Prevention of Terrorism (Additional Powers) Act 1996 which was announced in Parliament on 1 April 1996 and was enacted two days later. The provisions of this Act with regard to police powers is included within the text. At the time of completing the final manuscript for this book (24 April 1996), the Offensive Weapons Bill is currently before Parliament and its proposed provisions have also been included insofar as they affect the exercise of police powers.*

---

* This was enacted on 4th July 1996.

This book will hopefully provide a useful focus to an increasingly complex and important topic. Its principal aim is to introduce this study to a wide range of persons who are new to the subject. A list of recommended further reading is included at the back for those wishing to study police powers in greater depth.

Introduction

'I .... do solemnly and sincerely
declare and affirm that I will well and truly serve
our Sovereign Lady the Queen in the office of
Constable, without favour or affection, malice or
ill will; and that I will, to the best of my power
cause the peace to be kept and preserved, and
prevent all offences against the persons and
properties of Her Majesty's subjects and that while
I continue to hold the said office I will, to the best
of my skill and knowledge discharge all the duties
thereof faithfully according to law.'

The above constitutes the solemn declaration taken
by all those newly appointed to the office of constable
within England and Wales. This ceremony is known as
the 'attestation' which takes place before a Justice of the
Peace (either a magistrate, or an Assistant Commissioner
if taken in London). Exactly how this declaration is put
into practice will be examined in subsequent chapters.

On balance the modern police officer does not have
a vast number of powers over and above those held by
ordinary citizens, and those which are given constitute
essential tools in the execution of their duty. This is

largely due to the origins of policing in this country being rooted in the common law which has ensured greater legal parity between a constable and other citizens compared to many nations abroad. This feature has led to the English concept of 'policing by consent', which is much envied by those nations whose police do not enjoy such relative integration within their communities. It is largely for this reason that nearly all police forces throughout the globe are permanently para-military by nature and generally larger in size per head of population. A further distinction between foreign policing and our own domestic system is that this function in England and Wales is currently divided between 43 different police forces whereas policing abroad is usually under more direct and centralised control.

The general concept of policing is not new, in fact various forms of law-enforcement which were in the nature of policing have existed since early Saxon times. However, the first modern style professional police force was established by Statute in 1829 under the auspices of Sir Robert Peel and by 1856 all of England and Wales was covered by a network of police forces. Many believe that the main driving-force behind the 1829 Act was the appalling crime rate particularly in the capital city. While this was undoubtedly a major factor there was also another issue equal in importance, namely the increase in the level of public disorder that had escalated in the eighteenth and early nineteenth centuries.

Whilst the military were traditionally used to quell rioting in places like London and other big cities, there were serious disadvantages in using armed troops. First, long delays were often experienced in transporting troops from their respective barracks to the scene of public disorder. Secondly, the only forms of weaponry available were either bullets or bayonets which had drastic consequences. The new police were able to resolve both problems by using wooden truncheons to control riots, and by being deployed throughout London on a regular patrol basis they were able to disperse many unruly gatherings before they escalated into full-scale disorder.

Although often regarded with disdain and suspicion by both populace and even certain persons in authority in their very earliest days, the new police quickly gained the respect and affection still found in the majority of the public today. Some maintain that this effect is waning but, despite recent attacks on our existing policing system, this country still remains the envy of the world with regard to its systems of law enforcement.

One does not have to venture many miles from the shores of Britain to see the marked difference between generally accepted standards of police conduct abroad and those expected and largely fulfilled by the police here.

1

The Structure of Policing in England and Wales

As mentioned in the introduction there are currently 43 police forces in England and Wales, although there is provision for the amalgamation of forces which could result in a smaller number in the future. Nearly all are accountable to a local police authority which usually consists of 17 members comprised of three local magistrates, nine local councillors and five independent persons approved by the Home Secretary. The main exception to this rule is the Metropolitan Police Force in London. At present this force is not accountable to a police authority as such, but comes under the direct control of the Home Secretary who is ultimately responsible to Parliament for all policing throughout England and Wales. (The City of London Police are accountable to the Common Council of the City of London.) There are, however, plans to establish a London-wide advisory and overseeing body appointed by the Home Secretary, although this will not be a police authority comparable to those outside

London. This provision, together with recent changes to the structure and functions of police authorities, has been effected through the Police and Magistrates' Courts Act 1994. This Statute contains a number of other wide-ranging measures that are likely to significantly affect the system of policing in England and Wales in the near future.

Each police force is headed by a chief constable although the two London forces, namely the City of London and Metropolitan Police, each have a commissioner. The rank structures both within and outside London are depicted in Figure 1. The headquarters and local command structures of a typical provincial police force are represented in Figures 2 and 3.

One of many important features within our police service as distinct from the armed forces is that all senior ranks including the heads of individual police forces have progressed from the rank of constable initially. The first Metropolitan Police commissioner to have risen through all the ranks was Sir Joseph Simpson who took office in 1958 and this is now the normal procedure throughout all police forces in Britain. There is currently no direct entry route to the more senior ranks as occurs in the armed forces although there is an accelerated promotion scheme for suitable candidates via the police staff college, but all have to complete the initial two-year probationary period as constables before any such move is made.

The general entry requirements for the police service are contingent upon good health, character, education and appearance and also upon British nationality. There are also varying requirements in respect of height and age limits. The training of recruits requires about four to five months full-time attendance at one of several police training centres throughout the country. Training remains a prevalent feature through-out the two-year probationary period and takes the form of practical street experience under supervision interdispersed with further classroom instruction.

In terms of specialist opportunities the police service possibly has no parallel. A constable having satisfactorily completed his or her probationary period is given the opportunity to either continue working in uniform at local police station level or to enter at some stage in their career any of the following specialist areas: these include the Criminal Investigation Department, Traffic Department, Mounted Police, Dog Handlers, Youth and Community officers, Drugs Squad, VIP Protection, Special Branch, Internal Investigations, Public Order Control, and many more. Yet many prefer to remain as uniformed officers in the local police divisions, believing that work at this level can still provide all the variety and opportunities that specialist work can bring. There is, of course, considerable merit in this assertion although as a whole police work is equally dependent upon both specialist and 'routine' police duties. However, not-withstanding even the highest ranks in the police service, the numerous Acts of Parliament covering police powers refer to all police officers as holders of the office of 'constable' unless specific ranks are stipulated for procedural purposes.

Mention must be made of the voluntary, part-time section of the police service known as the Special Constabulary. Apart from the fact that its more modern version was instituted in 1831, just two years after the Metropolitan Police, its earliest beginnings supersede the regular force by many years. The Special Constabulary consists of part-time officers who perform police duties in their spare time and come from a wide variety of occupational backgrounds. Special constables have the same powers as their professional counterparts, therefore reference to a 'constable' throughout this book applies to specials as well as regular police officers of all ranks. See Figure 1 for the general grade structure of the Special Constabulary. (The reader is recommended to read an article written by the author of this book in *The Magistrate*, April 1991, 'The Special Constabulary – Asset or Anachronism?)

FIGURE 1

THE POLICE RANK STRUCTURE

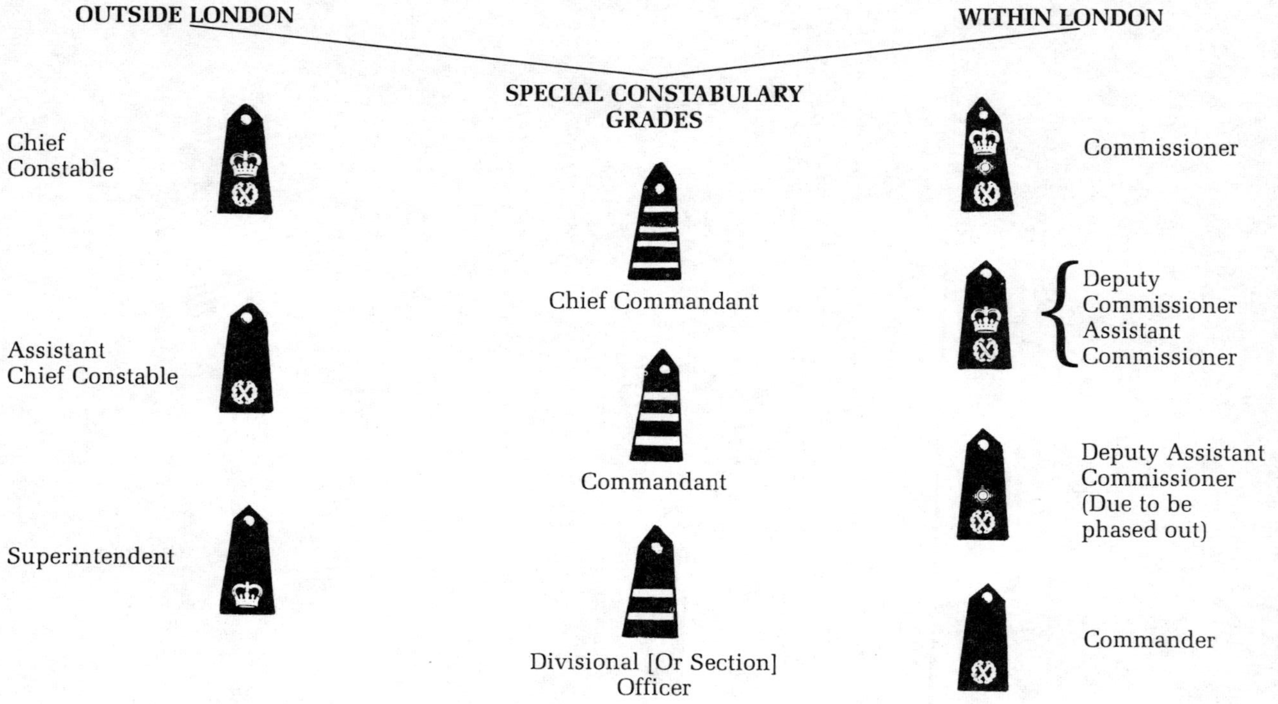

OUTSIDE LONDON

Chief
Constable

Assistant
Chief Constable

Superintendent

**SPECIAL CONSTABULARY
GRADES**

Chief Commandant

Commandant

Divisional [Or Section]
Officer

WITHIN LONDON

Commissioner

Deputy
Commissioner
Assistant
Commissioner

Deputy Assistant
Commissioner
(Due to be
phased out)

Commander

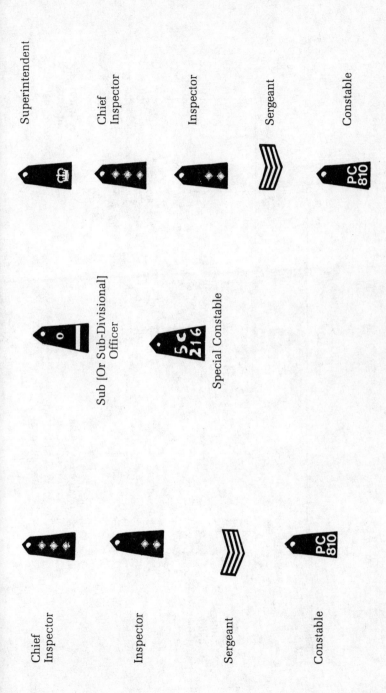

Superintendent

Chief
Inspector

Inspector

Sergeant

Constable

Chief
Inspector

Inspector

Sergeant

Constable

Sub [Or Sub-Divisional]
Officer

Special Constable

Note: The ranks of Chief Superintendent and Deputy Chief Constable are still technically being held by some of those who occupied these posts before they were abolished. These ranks will eventually disappear.

FIGURE 2

THE HEADQUARTERS COMMAND STRUCTURE OF A POLICE FORCE

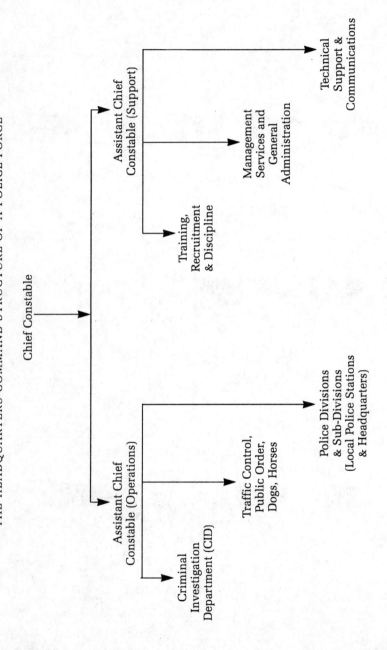

FIGURE 3

THE LOCAL COMMAND STRUCTURE OF A POLICE FORCE

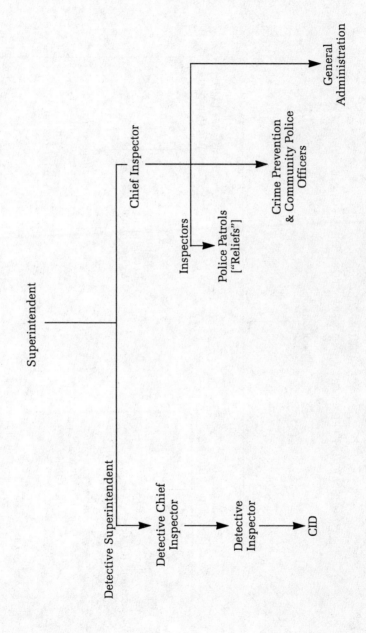

2

Police Powers to Stop and Search

INTRODUCTION

The main embodiment of police powers are now consolidated within the Police and Criminal Evidence Act 1984, supplemented by the latest Home Office Codes of Practice which became effective on 10 April 1995. The original version came into force on 1 January 1986 and the second edition took effect on 1 April 1991. The Codes of Practice are intended to clarify the 1984 Act and provide essential guidance for those who use its powers. However, a number of other powers are vested in the police and these originate from other Statutes and the common law which also include powers held by them as ordinary citizens. (See Figure 4). One of the more recent additions to the range of statutes which confer powers upon the police is the Criminal Justice and Public Order Act 1994. The latest Codes of Practice also provide guidance regarding the exercise of some of these additional powers which will be covered in this chapter and in other parts of the book.

Further powers were given to the police under the

Prevention of Terrorism (Additional Powers) Act 1996, and also the Offensive Weapons Bill is currently passing through Parliament which is intended to become law by the summer of 1996 and will provide further police powers. It is important at this stage to give the general definition of a police officer who is described as a citizen in uniform, and/or the holder of a warrant card, who is given certain additional powers in order that he or she may perform their duty.

In the following outline of police powers, all references to Sections are applicable to the Police and Criminal Evidence Act 1984 unless otherwise stated, and the Act itself will be referred to as 'PACE' which is the generally recognised term for the 1984 Act.

STOP AND SEARCH UNDER PACE

Under s1 if a constable has reasonable grounds to suspect that stolen or prohibited articles are being carried, that police officer may stop, detain and search persons or vehicles and seize such items (see Figure 5). Before proceeding further it is essential to consider what constitutes 'reasonable grounds to suspect' and 'prohibited articles' (stolen goods are largely self-explanatory and will therefore not be explained here).

REASONABLE GROUNDS TO SUSPECT

This phrase is only mentioned in PACE but is clarified in the Codes of Practice. Reasonable suspicion is defined in the latter as being an objective or tangible cause for suspicion on the part of the constable depending upon individual circumstances. While no comprehensive list of factors which would create reasonable suspicion exists, a number of guidelines have been given. These include general furtive behaviour and a person matching the description of a suspect from information received. It is stressed that these powers must not be used subjectively, such as stopping someone because of their colour, unorthodox appearance or even knowledge of any previous offences on their part. In short, there must be a tangible and positive condition present to justify the use of police powers to stop and search under s1. It should be noted that the police now have powers to stop and search under anti-terrorist legislation where such powers may be exercised without any pre-requisite suspicion. These new powers will be discussed later.

PROHIBITED ARTICLES

Under PACE prohibited articles can be placed into two general categories: namely, offensive weapons and articles which can be used for theft.

Offensive Weapons

An offensive weapon is defined as any article made or adapted to cause personal injury or any article intended to have this effect even if it has not been made or adapted for this purpose. The first category covers objects specifically manufactured for the sole purpose of causing injury such as knuckle-dusters, bayonets and sword-sticks. The second group includes articles made for an entirely innocent purpose that have been changed into a weapon such as a rolling-pin with one handle removed to be used as a cosh. The final category is concerned with items that fall under neither of the first two groups because they are neither manufactured or adapted weapons. Virtually any objects, such as combs, pens and keys, can fall under this heading provided there is intention to use them to cause personal injury.

Although treated separately under PACE, articles which constitute blades or sharp points will be included here for the sake of simplicity. Such items include any blade or article with a sharp point and folding knives unless the blade is less than three inches long when exposed. Under certain circumstances objects falling in this category may also be regarded as offensive weapons, hence their inclusion under this general heading. Offences under the Crossbows Act 1987 have also been included within the Codes of Practice which necessitate its inclusion here.

It should be noted at this juncture that a new power to stop and search persons for offensive weapons, including articles with blades or sharp points three inches or more when extended, is going to be introduced under the Offensive Weapons Bill. However, this proposed new power will only extend to school premises in addition to public places.

Articles for use in theft

These include objects which can also be used for stealing a motor vehicle, and obtaining property by deception and burglary. These have included a variety of house-breaking implements such as jemmies, screwdrivers, skeleton keys and less obvious articles such as adhesive tape and gloves.

Although the bulk of police powers to stop and search are contained within PACE, a number of other powers exist in Statutes enacted both before and after the 1984 Act (See Figure 4). These include the Public

Stores Act 1875, the Firearms Act 1968, the Misuse of Drugs Act 1971, the Customs and Excise Management Act 1979, the Aviation Security Act 1982, the Sporting Events (Control of Alcohol etc) Act 1985, the Crossbows Act 1987, the Prevention of Terrorism (Temporary Provisions) Act 1989, the Criminal Justice and Public Order Act 1994 and several Statutes designed to protect certain wildlife. The Codes of Practice apply to most Statutes that give the police powers to stop and search.

Under s1 the power to stop and search must be confined to public places. This does not mean that this must be confined only to the streets but includes places regarded as private property where the public have access such as car parks, cinemas, museums and public houses. If a building constitutes a dwelling, however, then these powers may only be exercised if the suspect does not live there and they do not have the permission of the occupier to be on the premises. This includes gardens or other land such as driveways or yards which are part of the dwelling, thereby preventing a suspect from running or driving into someone else's garden or yard, for instance, in order to avoid themselves or their motor vehicle being searched.

There are, of course, less formal and more subtle means available to confirm or repudiate any form of suspicion without the use of substantive powers to stop, detain and search. It is quite common for the police to speak to or question anyone on an informal basis in the course of their everyday duties, although there is no legal duty for citizens to answer questions put to them by the police as held in *Rice-v.-Connolly (1966)*. However, refusal to answer questions may reinforce an existing suspicion thereby enabling the police to draw upon their powers. It is important to distinguish between passive silence as in the latter case

15

and active non-cooperation as shown in *Ricketts-v.-Cox (1981)* where the suspect not only refused to answer questions put to him by the police in the street but became abusive and was subsequently convicted of wilfully obstructing them. It was also held in *Donnelly-v.-Jackman (1970)* that the police may take reasonable steps to attract attention such as tapping someone's shoulder in order to ask a question but they may not forcibly detain anyone in order to answer them as held in *Collins-v.-Wilcock (1984)*.

The Codes of Practice have included the requirement that in every instance where a suspect is to be searched for stolen property and/or prohibited articles, the suspect should be persuaded to voluntarily produce it even if there is an initial objection. Only if such cooperation is not forthcoming should a constable resort to their powers under s1. However, juveniles and other persons incapable of giving proper consent, which includes the mentally ill, should not be subject to a voluntary search.

A police officer exercising the power under s1 to search a suspect must naturally stop and detain the suspect initially but there must be reasonable grounds for suspicion beforehand. In other words a constable may not stop and detain in order to establish reasonable grounds for suspicion in order to search a suspect. It is sometimes unnecessary for the police to proceed beyond the stop or detention stage if it becomes apparent that stolen or prohibited articles are not being carried by a person or in a motor vehicle. This can occur as a result of satisfactory answers being given to questions, in which case the police do not have to proceed beyond any stage leading up to a search.

Under s2 if a search becomes necessary following the suspect or vehicle being stopped, the constable should state his or her name and station to which attached (if the constable is not in uniform this should be preceded by the showing of their warrant card). The police officer must then state the object and grounds for the search to the suspect or to the person in charge of the motor vehicle. With regard to the searching of motor vehicles, the initial stopping of a conveyance must be done by a police officer in uniform. However, a constable in plain clothes may search a motor vehicle if it has already stopped. Unattended vehicles may be searched but since the person in charge of it will not be present it is, of course, not possible to convey to that person the name of the officer, his or her station, and the object and grounds of the search. In such circumstances the constable should leave a notice identifying his or herself, the station to which attached, and information that the vehicle has been searched. Mention should be made that an application for compensation in respect of any damage caused by the search should be directed to the relevant police station. Under s3 the notice should conclude by stating that the person in charge of the vehicle or the owner may obtain a copy of the record covering the search within a period of one year. This will be completed by the officer carrying out the search either at the scene or as soon as possible after the incident. If a vehicle is searched and the person in charge of it is present at the time, he or she should also be made aware of the availability of a record covering the incident, a copy of which may be obtained within a year. The same rule applies to pedestrians who are searched.

S3 also states that a record of the search need not be compiled if it is impracticable to do so. This will apply if, for instance, a large number of people are searched in a short space of time or even where one suspect is searched but the constable cannot remain at the scene any longer due to an urgent call elsewhere. This same Section provides that if a person who is searched fails to provide their name the constable may not detain them for this purpose and that a description of the suspect will suffice.

S2 states the extent to which a suspect may be searched in a public place which must be confined to a superficial examination or removal of certain outer clothing only. This excludes footwear and headgear, although it should be noted that this does not apply with regard to the exercise of police powers to prevent acts of terrorism (see below). Any further examination should be conducted in private, such as in a police van, but strip searching may only be carried out at a police station following the arrest of the suspect and under very strict rules as stipulated in s55. Under s117 a police officer may use reasonable force to exercise his or her powers under the relevant Sections in PACE, including the power to stop and search. However, more than slight resistance could result in the suspect being arrested for wilfully resisting or obstructing or even assaulting police and sometimes public order offences may be committed. S1 states that any items believed to be stolen property or prohibited articles may be seized by the police and, of course, this will be followed by the arrest of the person from whom such items were found either on their person or the motor vehicle in which they were an occupant.

POWERS TO STOP/SEARCH VEHICLES AND FURTHER POWERS TO STOP/SEARCH PEDESTRIANS

The police have a number of powers to stop motor vehicles under the common law and Statute. Probably the most frequently used is s163 of the Road Traffic Act 1988 which gives a constable the power to stop any motor vehicle for a variety of reasons, although usually this is confined to road traffic offences such as the need to check on driving documents or the vehicle's general condition. However, s4 of PACE enables the police to organise road blocks using the power of s163 if a serious arrestable offence has been, or is likely to be committed (the definition of a serious arrestable offence will be covered in Chapter 5), or it is necessary to use this means to trace witnesses to a serious arrestable offence or apprehend a person unlawfully at large. The authorisation of road blocks must be made in writing by a police officer of at least the rank of superintendent and such authority lasts for 7 days but is renewable. In an emergency a police officer of lower rank may act in this capacity but is under a duty to inform a superintendent or above as soon as possible. The police may also rely on their powers under common law to stop motor vehicles to prevent a breach of the peace, such as in *Moss-v.-McLachlan (1985)* where it was held lawful for the police to set up road blocks to prevent pickets reaching their destinations during the miners' strike of 1984/5.

POWERS UNDER THE CRIMINAL JUSTICE AND PUBLIC ORDER ACT 1994 AND THE PREVENTION OF TERRORISM (ADDITIONAL POWERS) ACT 1996

The Criminal Justice and Public Order Act 1994 provides the police with several new powers to stop motor vehicles (and pedestrians). Section 60 empowers the police in uniform to stop and search any vehicle and persons in it (or persons on foot), for offensive

19

weapons or dangerous instruments, and to seize any such articles subsequently found. This power may be exercised whether or not there are any grounds for suspecting that such articles are being carried (note the contrast with s1 of PACE). However, such powers may only be exercised if a superintendent or above (or an inspector or chief inspector in an emergency), has given written authorisation for such powers to be exercised in anticipation of serious violence. This authorisation cannot exceed 24 hours duration (but can be extended for a further six hours), and it must specify the area under which these powers may be used (see Figure 6).

Section 81 of the 1994 Act [as amended by s1 of the Prevention of Terrorism (Additional Powers) Act 1996)], empowers an assistant chief constable (outside London) or a commander (the equivalent rank within the London area), or above, to give an authorisation in writing for uniformed officers within his area to stop any vehicle (or pedestrian), to search any vehicle and its occupants, (or anything on or carried by a pedestrian), for articles which could be used in terrorism. As with s60 above, these stop and search powers may be exercised even of the police officers at the scene do not have any grounds for suspecting that such articles are being carried (see Figure 7). However, the amended section 81 enables the police to remove headgear and footwear in the course of a search as well as an outer coat, jacket or gloves where necessary.

The latest Codes of Practice provide important guidelines in view of the potentially wide scope of the powers under s60 (and the original s81) of the 1994 Act. The Codes stress the need for these powers to be exercised objectively, and go on to advise authorising officers to set the minimum with regard to the duration and geographical areas covering the exercise of these powers. The general conduct of stops and searches under s60 (and the original s81), fall broadly under the same guidelines as those pertaining to s1 of PACE and it is anticipated that this will also apply to the amended s81, including the new power to remove any headgear and footwear, as well as other new powers under recent anti-terrorist legislation. In due course new Codes of Practice will be published which will specifically cover the exercise of all the relevant police powers.

Further powers to stop persons are contained under sections 65 and 71 of the Criminal Justice and Public Order Act 1994. In both cases these powers are intended to prevent persons going to certain gatherings. Section 65 provides uniformed police officers with the power to stop persons reasonably believed to be travelling to a 'rave' where it has already been disbanded under the direction of a superintendent or above. This power may only be exercised within a five mile radius of the gathering and the police have a further power to direct the persons stopped not to proceed in the direction of the 'rave'. Section 71 is identical to s65 except that it relates to the prevention of persons reasonably believed to be going to the venue of a prohibited assembly.

A number of restrictions, where necessary, upon the movement of pedestrians and vehicles have been enacted under s4 and Schedule 6A and also s5 of the Prevention of Terrorism (Additional Powers) Act 1996. Under s4 and Schedule 6A (see Figure 8), a police superintendent or above (or an officer below this rank in a matter of great urgency), may authorise a cordon to be imposed within a stated area for an initial period of 14 days. This may only be done where it is expedient to do so in connection with a terrorist investigation. When a cordon is in force, the police may order anyone within it to leave even if they are in premises at the time, and drivers/persons in charge of vehicles must remove them from the area if so ordered. The police may also prohibit or restrict any access to a cordoned area to pedestrians and vehicles, and any vehicle within the cordoned area may be repositioned by the police either within or outside the restricted area. (See Chapter 3 for search powers pertaining to premises under s4 and Schedule 6A to the 1996 Act).

Finally, under s5 of the 1996 Act, a commander or assistant chief constable may authorise the prohibition or restriction of parking on specified roads for an initial 28 day period. Such authorisation may only be given where it is expedient in order to prevent acts of terrorism.

FIGURE 4

SOME SOURCES OF POLICE POWERS

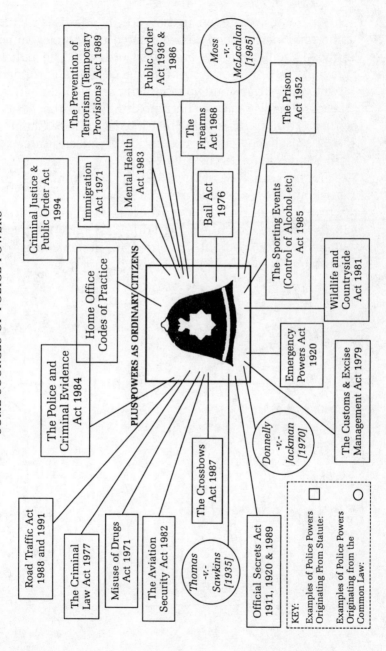

PLUS POWERS AS ORDINARY/CITIZENS

Criminal Justice & Public Order Act 1994

The Prevention of Terrorism (Temporary Provisions) Act 1989

Public Order Act 1936 & 1986

Immigration Act 1971

Mental Health Act 1983

The Firearms Act 1968

Moss -v.- McLachlan [1985]

Home Office Codes of Practice

Bail Act 1976

The Prison Act 1952

The Police and Criminal Evidence Act 1984

The Sporting Events (Control of Alcohol etc) Act 1985

Wildlife and Countryside Act 1981

Emergency Powers Act 1920

Road Traffic Act 1988 and 1991

The Customs & Excise Management Act 1979

The Criminal Law Act 1977

Misuse of Drugs Act 1971

The Aviation Security Act 1982

The Crossbows Act 1987

Donnelly -v.- Jackman [1970]

Thomas -v.- Sawkins [1935]

Official Secrets Act 1911, 1920 & 1989

KEY:

Examples of Police Powers Originating From Statute: ☐

Examples of Police Powers Originating from the Common Law: ◯

FIGURE 5

POLICE POWERS TO STOP, DETAIN & SEARCH UNDER S1 OF PACE

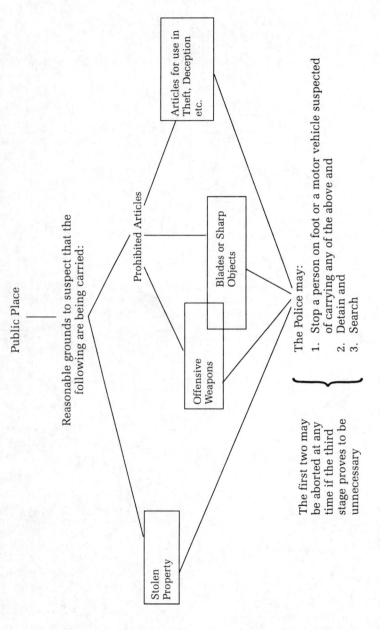

FIGURE 6

POLICE POWERS TO STOP AND SEARCH UNDER S60 OF
THE CRIMINAL JUSTICE AND PUBLIC ORDER ACT 1994
(in anticipation of serious violence)

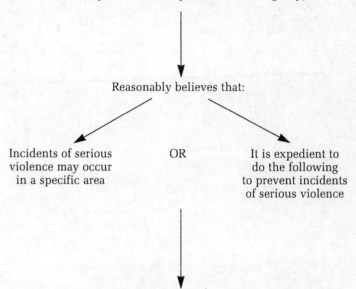

If a superintendent or above
(or an inspector/chief inspector in an emergency):

Reasonably believes that:

Incidents of serious   OR   It is expedient to
violence may occur   do the following
in a specific area   to prevent incidents
of serious violence

That officer may give written authorisation for uniformed
police officers to stop/search vehicles/persons within a
specified area and time (no more than 24 hours, extendable
by a further 6 hours)

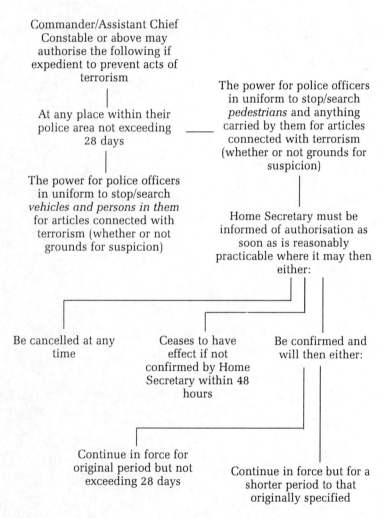

FIGURE 7

POLICE POWERS TO STOP/SEARCH UNDER S81
(AS AMENDED) OF THE CRIMINAL JUSTICE AND PUBLIC
ORDER ACT 1994 AND S1 OF THE PREVENTION OF
TERRORISM (ADDITIONAL POWERS) ACT 1996
(Consolidated under Sections 13a and 13b of the Prevention of Terrorism
[Temporary Provisions] Act 1989)

Commander/Assistant Chief Constable or above may authorise the following if expedient to prevent acts of terrorism

At any place within their police area not exceeding 28 days

The power for police officers in uniform to stop/search *vehicles and persons in them* for articles connected with terrorism (whether or not grounds for suspicion)

The power for police officers in uniform to stop/search *pedestrians* and anything carried by them for articles connected with terrorism (whether or not grounds for suspicion)

Home Secretary must be informed of authorisation as soon as is reasonably practicable where it may then either:

Be cancelled at any time

Ceases to have effect if not confirmed by Home Secretary within 48 hours

Be confirmed and will then either:

Continue in force for original period but not exceeding 28 days

Continue in force but for a shorter period to that originally specified

26

FIGURE 8

POLICE CORDONS

Superintendent or above may authorise a cordon to be imposed within a specified area if expedient to do so in connection with an investigation into terrorism ◄----- Police officers below the rank of superintendent may authorise a cordon if the matter is of great urgency, but must inform a superintendent or above as soon as is reasonably practicable who may either confirm or cancel it.

Initial authorisation must not exceed 14 days (renewable for overall period not exceeding 28 days)

Police officers at the scene have powers to:

| Order persons to leave the cordoned area including persons in buildings | Order persons in charge of vehicles to remove them | Reposition any vehicle | Prohibit or restrict any vehicular or pedestrian access |

Superintendent or above may authorise police officers within the area of a cordon to do the following if reasonable grounds for believing material likely to be of substantial value to a terrorist investigation is likely to be found on premises within the cordoned area (excluding items subject to legal privilege, excluded or special procedure material)

Search premises specified in the authorisation and any person found there.

Seize and retain anything found if reasonable grounds for believing it is likely to be of substantial value to the terrorist investigation and it is necessary to prevent it from being concealed, lost, damaged, altered or destroyed (except items subject to legal privilege)

27

3

Police Powers of Entry and Search of Premises

For the purposes of police powers, the word 'premises' includes a wide variety of public and private places including buildings, caravans, houseboats, tents, vehicles, vessels such as aircraft, non-residential premises such as unattended garages, and sometimes land. The two main forms of entry, search (and seizure) by police in premises are those conducted with or without a warrant.

ENTRY AND SEARCH BY WARRANT

Over the years a number of Acts of Parliament have been passed giving the police powers to enter and search premises under the authority of a warrant. These include searches for drugs, firearms, stolen goods and explosives to name but a few. PACE has now introduced a standard procedure for obtaining warrants under the relevant Statutes and also provides magistrates with a general power to issue warrants to search for items not covered by the various Acts. S8 provides that a police officer may apply for a warrant from a magistrate if there are reasonable grounds for believing that there is evidence on premises relating to the committing of a serious arrestable offence (see Chapter 5), and that this is the only means to obtain such evidence. Therefore a magistrate should not issue a warrant if entry can be gained through the consent of the occupier. Certain objects may not be obtained under a warrant. These are items subject to legal privilege, excluded material or special procedure material.

Items subject to legal privilege include communications between a qualified lawyer and his or her client; excluded material includes personal records of a commercial or professional nature such as medical records. Certain specimens for medical diagnosis are also included under excluded material as is journalistic material held in confidence. Special procedure material includes such items as company accounts and other confidential information of a commercial nature such as a proposed new product or expansion pro-gramme. The police may still obtain evidence in the form of excluded or special procedure material by applying to a circuit judge for a production order or in extreme cases a warrant may be obtained from the same source. Material which is legally privileged cannot be obtained by warrant although, for instance, under the Official Secrets Act 1911 a police superintendent can give written authority to search in cases of serious emergency.

ENTRY AND SEARCH WITHOUT WARRANT

With the exception of police powers to prevent or generally deal with a breach of the peace, all other common law powers of entry were abolished by PACE. However, a number of Statutes passed before and after PACE enable police entry into premises without warrant in addition to the powers contained within the 1984 Act. In the latter instance powers of entry without warrant are contained within ss17, 18 and 32.

POWERS OF ENTRY AND SEARCH UNDER S17

Apart from powers contained in the miscellaneous Statutes mentioned above, under s17 any police officer may enter and search premises for the purpose of executing an arrest warrant or a warrant of commitment. The latter refers to the failure to pay money ordered in a magistrates' court such as a maintenance or compensation order or a fine. S17 also includes entering and searching premises in order to make an arrest for an arrestable offence, make an arrest under s1 of the Public Order Act 1936, ss6 to 8, or 10 of the Criminal Law Act 1977 or s4 of the Public Order Act 1986. Entry and search for the purposes of detaining persons unlawfully at large or preventing endangerment to life and limb or serious damage to property are also included under the provisions of s17 (the former power has been strengthened by the Prisoners [Return to Custody] Act 1995). It is important to note that this Section only gives the police the power to search in pursuit of their intended purpose. In other words they may only look for persons in places likely to contain a human being, or objects in places where they are likely to be found. It would therefore be contrary to s17 for instance to rifle through a filing cabinet while in pursuit of an escaped prisoner.

POWERS OF ENTRY AND SEARCH UNDER S18

These provisions cover entry and search following the arrest of a person for an arrestable offence who occupies or controls the premises in question in order to find further evidence. If the suspect is already at the police station the written authority of at least an inspector is necessary to invoke s18, whereas if the suspect is detained at a place other than a police station any police officer may enter the premises and conduct a search but must inform the relevant senior officer as soon as possible after the event. Either way that senior police officer must make a full record of the search.

POWERS OF ENTRY AND SEARCH UNDER S32

Under this Section the police may enter and search any premises if a suspect arrested away from a police station was either in those premises at the time of the arrest or was there just prior to being arrested. This is for the purpose of enabling them to search for any evidence if they reasonably believe that it will be found there. The search must be limited to the extent of what the police anticipate finding and it is not necessary for the premises to be owned, occupied or controlled by the suspect.

A number of safeguards regarding powers of entry and search are specified within the Codes of Practice. These include confining such activities to reasonable times of the day or night, ensuring minimum disturbance to occupants, informing local police liaison officers if entry and search is likely to have an adverse effect on relations between the police and the community, and attempting to communicate with the person entitled to grant access in order to seek cooperation in gaining entry. Certain safeguards may be waived if it is believed that such measures would obstruct the purpose of the entry and search, and s117 provides that reasonable force may be used where necessary.

The Codes of Practice also provide that where searches may be carried out with the consent of a person entitled to do so, this consent should be obtained in writing wherever possible.

POWERS UNDER THE PREVENTION OF
TERRORISM (ADDITIONAL POWERS) ACT 1996

The 1996 Act has introduced a number of additional police powers to search premises. Section 2 enables a superintendent, or above, to apply to a magistrate for a warrant to enter and search one or more non-residential premises if there are reasonable grounds for believing that material will be found there which will assist in a terrorist investigation. This excludes items subject to legal privilege, or excluded or special procedure material. This power enables a warrant to be obtained covering more than one building such as a block of lock-up garages, whereas the pre-existing powers necessitated each location being named. Entry and search must be effected within 24 hours of the warrant being issued, and in cases of great urgency such searches may be effected without a warrant on the authority of a superintendent or above. Persons found on these premises may also be searched.

Section 4 and Schedule 6A of the 1996 Act (see Figure 8), enable premises to be searched whilst a police cordon is in effect. During such time a police officer of at least the rank of superintendent, may give written authority for any premises which are wholly or partly within the cordon to be searched and anyone found there. Such authorisations may be given if there are reasonable grounds for believing that material is likely to be found there which will assist in a terrorist investigation (except items subject to legal privilege or excluded or special procedure material). Entry may be effected at any time the cordon is in operation and on more than one occasion. If any person is found on the premises and subsequently searched *in public*, the police may remove any headgear, footwear, outer coat, jacket or gloves. This is a further example of where headgear and footwear may be removed in public where the police are acting under certain prevention of terrorism legislation.

Proposed powers under the Offensive Weapons Bill

The Offensive Weapons Bill, when enacted, will provide the police with the power to enter school premises (using reasonable force if necessary) and search them and any person on them for offensive weapons and articles with blades or points. The exercise of this power will be contingent upon the officer having reasonable grounds for believing that such items are, or have been, unlawfully carried. The term 'school premises' means land and buildings used for school purposes but excludes dwellings used by persons employed at schools. This will cover the homes of school employees such as caretakers and grounds-men for instance. Colleges of further and higher education as well as universities will not fall within the scope of this power since it applies only to educational institutions providing primary or secondary education.

4

Police Powers of Seizure

A number of Sections under PACE have given the police further specific and general powers to seize property, and a number of Statutes passed both before and after PACE give the police a variety of powers of seizure in respect of certain categories of property. These include the Betting, Gaming and Lotteries Act 1963, the Biological Weapons Act 1974, the Criminal Damage Act 1971, the Misuse of Drugs Act 1971, the Theft Act 1968, the Financial Services Act 1986, the Drug Trafficking Act 1994 and the Criminal Justice and Public Order Act 1994 to name but a few.

GENERAL POWERS OF SEIZURE UNDER PACE, OTHER STATUTES AND THE COMMON LAW

A constable may seize anything if he or she has reasonable grounds for believing that it constitutes evidence in relation to any offence or it has been obtained as a result of an offence being committed and that it is necessary to seize such items to prevent them being hidden, lost, changed or destroyed. Material subject to legal privilege may not be seized under any power conferred under PACE or any other Statute. The general power of seizure only applies when the constable is on the premises lawfully namely if he or she is executing a search warrant or any other search under written authority, is dealing with or preventing a breach of the peace, entering premises under ss17, 18 or 32 (see Chapter Three), or has entered with the consent of a person entitled to give it.

SPECIFIC POWERS OF SEIZURE UNDER PACE

Property may be seized by the police under the following circumstances:

Articles obtained as a result of a search under s1 which are believed to be stolen or prohibited; anything obtained as a result of a warrant issued by magistrates under s8 regarding evidence of a serious arrestable offence or anything obtained in the execution of a search warrant authorised by a circuit judge; any object found as a result of searches under ss18 and 32 (power to search premises after an arrest); and anything found under ss54 and 55 as a result of the search of a suspect while detained by the police (see Chapter 5).

SPECIFIC POWERS OF SEIZURE UNDER THE CRIMINAL JUSTICE AND PUBLIC ORDER ACT 1994

Section 60 (6) provides the police with the power to seize any offensive or dangerous weapons found in the course of a search under written authority in anticipation of serious violence (see Chapter 2). Under s64(4), the police may seize vehicles and/or sound equipment used for 'raves' under certain circumstances, and s62 provides the power to seize vehicles which have not been removed from land in accordance with a direction under s61 (power to remove trespassers on land).

SPECIFIC POWERS OF SEIZURE UNDER THE PREVENTION OF TERRORISM (ADDITIONAL POWERS) ACT 1996

The police are provided with the power to seize and retain items (except those subject to legal privilege) in non-residential premises and from persons on such premises, which are found in the course of a search under s2 of the 1996 Act (see Chapter 3). This may be done if any item is reasonably believed to be of substantial value to a terrorist investigation and that it is necessary to prevent it from being concealed, lost, damaged, altered or destroyed.

Under Schedule 6A to the 1996 Act, which is linked with s4, the police may seize and retain anything found on premises or on any person found there which are within a police cordon and are subject to a search under written authority by a superintendent or above (see also Chapter 3). Any property seized must not be subject to legal privilege and it must be reasonably believed that it is likely to be of substantial value to a terrorist investigation and seizure is necessary to prevent its concealment, loss, damage, alteration or destruction.

PROPOSED POWERS UNDER THE OFFENSIVE WEAPONS BILL

Police officers using the proposed power to search school premises and persons on them for offensive weapons and articles with blades or points (see Chapter 3), may seize and retain such articles if found there.

5

Police Powers of Arrest

An arrest may now be defined as the lawful deprivation of a citizen's liberty, exercised in what ever degree is reasonably necessary in order to assist in the investigation of an alleged crime, or ensure that the accused is brought before a court, or to preserve the safety of the accused or others or their property, or to be finger-printed. Prior to the passing of PACE an arrest was simply a means to bring a suspect to court but there are provisions under ss25 and 27 of the Act that now enable a constable to arrest for other reasons.

PACE, among a number of other things, rationalised many statutory police powers of arrest that existed prior to its passing and all such powers now work through it, although a number of Statutes containing powers of arrest are still preserved. Since the enactment of PACE other Statutes have also been passed giving further arrest powers to the police, such as the Sporting Events (Control of Alcohol etc) Act 1985, the Public Order Act 1986 and the Criminal Justice and Public Order Act 1994. The only common law power of arrest to survive PACE is the power of arrest necessary to prevent or deal with a breach of the peace. This is held by both ordinary citizens and the police.

There are two forms of arrest, namely those executed under warrant and those without warrant. Arrests under warrant account for the minority of arrests in total especially since the introduction of PACE. The most prolific warrants are those issued under the Magistrates' Courts Act 1980 which can be issued against any adult who is suspected of having, or has committed an imprisonable offence, or whose whereabouts are unknown. This Statute also enables Bench Warrants to be issued against persons who fail to appear in court having been initially served with a summons.

Warrants are issued either with the provision for bail or may not provide bail at all. The latter is usual where Bench Warrants are issued since the arrest is necessary because the accused has failed to appear in court when required.

The police have many powers to arrest without warrant, a number of which are also held by ordinary citizens. A summary of police powers of arrest in this respect is as follows: Arrestable (and serious arrestable) offences defined in ss24 and 116 respectively; non-arrestable offences which meet the special requirements under s25 (known as 'general arrest conditions'); breach of the peace at common law; offences covered by Statutes passed prior to and preserved by PACE, and Statutes enacted subsequent to PACE; and arrest in order to be fingerprinted under s27 (See Figure 9).

ARRESTABLE (AND SERIOUS ARRESTABLE) OFFENCES

S24 defines arrestable offences as follows: offences where the sentence is fixed by law, namely murder and treason where only the life sentence may be imposed; offences where a person of at least 21 years may be sentenced to a term of five years imprisonment on a first conviction; then miscellaneous offences as follows: offences under the Customs and Excise Acts; offences under the Official Secrets Acts of 1920 and 1989; two offences under the Sexual Offences Act 1956; two offences under the Theft Act 1968; any offence under the Football (Offences) Act 1991; publishing/distributing racially inflammatory material; ticket and taxi touting; possession of an offensive weapon/article with blade or point in a public place or in school premises* also conspiring, inciting, aiding, abetting, counselling or procuring any of the above, and attempting with the exception of one offence under the Theft Act 1968.**

S24 goes on to define the powers of arrest conferred upon both police and ordinary citizens. For simplicity's sake these complex rules are illustrated in Figure 9 and summarised as follows: Anyone may summarily arrest (arrest without warrant) any person who *is actually committing* an arrestable offence or where there are reasonable grounds for suspecting that they are committing an arrestable offence, or any person who is guilty of *having* committed an arrestable offence or there are reasonable grounds to suspect that they have done so. The police are empowered under PACE to go further than the latter since they may arrest even if they only have reasonable cause to suspect that an arrestable offence has been committed in the first place. The police may also arrest any person who is *about to* commit an arrestable offence or any person who they have reasonable cause to suspect of being

---

*   This arrest power is proposed under the Offensive Weapons Bill.

**   It seems unclear whether this also applies to ticket and taxi touting which are summary offences only.

about to commit an arrestable offence. This power is not held by ordinary citizens under PACE although under s3 of the Criminal Law Act 1967 all persons may use reasonable force to prevent crime, effect or assist in the lawful arrest of offenders or suspects, or persons unlawfully at large.

Serious arrestable offences are treated no differently to arrestable offences in respect of actually arresting suspects. The distinction between the two is necessary for other procedures such as authorising road checks, the taking of intimate samples from suspects and periods of detention without charge (see Chapter 6). The definition of serious arrestable offences in PACE is complex, but for simplicity offences falling under this heading can be divided into two categories as follows:

CRIMES WHICH ARE ALWAYS SERIOUS ARRESTABLE OFFENCES

Treason, murder, manslaughter, rape, kidnapping, incest with a girl under 13, buggery with a boy under 16 or with anyone who did not consent, indecent assault in the form of gross indecency, causing an explosion likely to endanger life, intercourse with a girl under 13, possession of a firearm with the intention to commit criminal offences, causing death through dangerous driving, hostage taking and hijacking, torture, certain drug trafficking offences, offences under the Prevention of Terrorism (Temporary Provisions) Act 1989 and obscenity offences and child pornography (except simple possession of material), are always serious arrestable offences with regard to the detention of suspects.

ARRESTABLE OFFENCES THAT MAY BECOME SERIOUS ARRESTABLE OFFENCES

Under s116 an arrestable offence may be transformed into a serious arrestable offence if any of the following conditions apply to it: Serious harm to State security or public order, serious interference with the administration of justice generally or with a particular case, any person's death or serious injury, or substantial financial gain or loss.

If an arrestable offence entails making a threat which is likely to lead to any of the above consequences then it will be regarded as a serious arrestable offence.

GENERAL ARREST CONDITIONS UNDER S25

This was a particularly controversial aspect of PACE during its passage through Parliament since it empowers the police to arrest anyone even if they have committed an offence which is not arrestable. On the surface this would appear to be a draconian power but deeper analysis into the purposes behind this provision discloses both good administrative intentions and humanitarian motives.

Non-arrestable offences include literally dozens of crimes which are usually regarded as relatively minor offences and the vast majority are dealt with at summary level before magistrates. These include nearly all motoring offences, common law assault, highway obstruction, dropping litter, and many more. The usual procedure for prosecuting offenders under this category is to issue a summons to attend court but its effectiveness is contingent upon the correct name and address being given. In the past, substantial numbers of summonses were returned unserved often due to incorrect particulars being given to the police at the scene. S25 now enables the police to arrest a person in connection with a non-arrestable offence which is being or has been committed or attempted if the constable believes the wrong name and/or address are being furnished or that the name given cannot be verified by the constable. The police may also arrest under these conditions if the address given is unsuitable for the service of a summons. This will apply, for example, if the suspect is clearly of no fixed abode and gives the address of a temporary overnight hostel. S25 also applies to situations where a suspect refuses to give their name and address. The constable may then arrest that person for both the offence in question and refusing to identify his or herself. If the suspect decides to cooperate before reaching the police station, however, s30 enables the police to release that person once they have satisfactorily identified themselves. This is effectively a power to de-arrest someone if there are no longer sufficient grounds to take them to a police station.

Further powers under s25 apply in cases where a non-arrestable offence is being or has been committed or attempted and it is reasonably believed necessary for a constable to arrest in order to prevent the suspect from: causing any physical injury to his or herself or others; being physically injured by others; causing loss or damage to property; committing an offence against public decency; causing unlawful highway obstruction; harming a child or other vulnerable person. These measures can therefore be regarded as preventive arrests.

COMMON LAW ARREST FOR A BREACH
OF THE PEACE

This is the only common law power of arrest that was left intact by PACE and it is held by both the police and ordinary citizens. A breach of the peace is defined as harm done or likely to be done to a person or to his property whilst he is present, or putting a person in fear of violence generally. The police may enter both public places and private property to prevent a breach of the peace and arrest any person who is believed will cause a breach, is causing a breach or who has just committed a breach of the peace and it is likely to recur. The power of the police to both enter, remain and generally deal with or prevent a breach of the peace is enshrined in a number of cases which include *Thomas-v.-Sawkins (1935), R-v.-Howell (1982), Lamb-v.-DPP (1989)* and *McConnell-v.-Chief Constable of the Greater Manchester Police (1990).*

It should be noted that a host of Statutory powers of entry and arrest exist to enable the police to deal with breaches of the peace such as in s17 of PACE and in a number of provisions under the Public Order Act 1986.

OTHER STATUTORY POWERS OF ARREST

As mentioned earlier in this chapter although PACE rationalised many earlier Statutes governing police powers of arrest, the 1984 Act did not eradicate all of them. Also a number of Statutes have been passed since PACE giving the police further powers of arrest. Examples of the former include Sections under the Military Lands Act 1892, the Protection of Animals Act 1911, the Emergency Powers Act 1920, the Public Order

Act 1936, the Prison Act 1952, the Street Offences Act 1959, the Immigration Act 1971, the Bail Act 1976, the Criminal Law Act 1977 and the Mental Health Act 1983. Examples of Acts passed subsequent to PACE mentioned earlier are the Sporting Events (Control of Alcohol etc) Act 1985, the Public Order Act 1986, the Criminal Justice and Public Order Act 1994 and the Prevention of Terrorism (Additional Powers) Act 1996. Police powers of arrest also exist under the Road Traffic Act 1988 regarding persons driving under the influence of drink or drugs, driving while disqualified and causing death through dangerous driving.

S27 ARREST WITHOUT WARRANT FOR FINGERPRINTING

Anyone who has been convicted of an offence where fingerprints are required and has not already been in police custody and his or her fingerprints have not already been taken in connection with the offence, may be required to attend a police station to have them taken. Failure to attend when required will give a constable the power to arrest that person in order to bring them to a police station to be fingerprinted.

This provision is intended to be used in instances where the accused has committed a recordable offence but has been brought to court by way of summons.

ARREST PROCEDURES

When arresting someone, either with or without a warrant, a constable must inform that individual that he or she is being arrested and state the reason. If that is not possible the person should be informed as soon as is practicable after the event. These rules are given under s28 which, if not complied with, may render the arrest unlawful. Under the Codes of Practice, the arresting officer should then administer the caution. Prior to the Criminal Justice and Public Order Act 1994, the wording used to be 'You do not have to say anything unless you wish to do so, but anything you do say may be given in evidence'. Since the implementation of this aspect of the 1994 Act on 10 April 1995, the wording of the caution is now: 'You do not have to say anything. But it may harm your defence if you do not mention when questioned something which you later rely on in court. Anything you do say may be given in evidence.'

S29 covers arrests made while the suspect is already at a police station but prior to that stage has attended voluntarily and s30 is concerned with arrests away from police stations where the majority of arrests take place. The main provision under s30 is the general requirement to take the suspect to a police station as soon as is practicable following an arrest.

It is important to mention s32 which gives a constable the power to search an arrested suspect away from a police station. This is distinct from the power to search persons or property when an arrest has not been made as discussed earlier. A constable may search a suspect who has been arrested at a place other than a police station if there are reasonable grounds to believe that the suspect has anything on their person with which they could harm themselves or others. This will also apply if it is reasonably believed that the suspect may be carrying anything which could be used to effect their escape or may have an object which constitutes evidence of a crime, but s32 may not be used to establish the suspect's identity. Under s117 reasonable force may be used to effect an arrest where necessary.

FIGURE 9

POWERS OF ARREST WITHOUT WARRANT
S24 OF POLICE AND CRIMINAL EVIDENCE ACT 1984

ALL CITIZENS (INCLUDING THE POLICE)

POLICE ONLY

MAY ARREST ANYONE:

Suspect caught in the act
{ Actually committing an arrestable offence or there are reasonable grounds for suspecting to be committing an arrestable offence

These conditions apply also to the police

OR

Suspect caught after the act
{ Anyone who is guilty of having committed an arrestable offence or there are reasonable grounds for suspecting this

These conditions apply also to the police

Or only reasonable grounds to suspect that an arrestable offence has been committed in the first place

Suspect caught before the act
{ No power for ordinary citizen to arrest under PACE although s3 of the Criminal Law Act 1967 gives both citizens and the police power to use reasonable force to prevent crime, etc.

May arrest anyone about to commit an arrestable offence or has reasonable grounds for suspecting they are about to do so.

Arrestable Offences [s24]

Offences where sentence fixed by law, offences where a person 21 years or over may be given a five year term of imprisonment on a first conviction, offences under the Customs and Excise Acts, the Official Secrets Acts 1920 & 1989, two offences under the Sexual Offences Act 1956, two offences under the Theft Act 1968. Any offence under the Football (Offences) Act 1991, publishing or distributing racially inflamatory material, possession of an offensive weapon or article with blade or sharp point in a public place or school premises*, ticket and taxi touting, also conspiring, inciting, aiding, abetting, counselling or procuring any of the foregoing, and attempting, except one offence under the Theft Act 1968.**

* Proposed under the Offensive Weapons Bill.
** It seems unclear whether this also applies to ticket/ taxi touting.

Can be transformed into serious arrestable offences under s116 if: Serious harm to state security or public order, serious interference with the administration of justice, or substantial financial gain or loss.

Crimes which are always classed as serious arrestable offences

Treason, murder, manslaughter, rape, kidnapping, incest with girl under 13, buggery with boy under 16 or with anyone not consenting, indecent assault in form of gross indecency, causing explosion likely to endanger life, intercourse with girl under 13, possession of firearm intending to commit criminal offences, causing death through dangerous driving, hostage-taking, hi-jacking, torture, certain drug trafficking offences, and offences under the Prevention of Terrorism (Temporary Provisions) Act 1989. Also, obscenity offences and child pornography (except simple possession of material).

These conditions apply also to the police.

General arrest conditions under S25 covers non-arrestable offences already committed, being committed or attempted where: name and address refused or not believed or verified, or if address unsuitable for service of a summons. Also if reasonable grounds to believe necessary to prevent injury to suspect or others or their property, committing offence against public decency, unlawful highway obstruction or harm to a child or other vulnerable person.

Other statutory powers of arrest preserved by PACE or passed since the 1984 Act.

Arrest without warrant for fingerprinting.

Common law arrest for a Breach of the Peace

No such powers are vested in the ordinary citizen

These powers are not given to the ordinary citizen

6

Police Powers to Detain

S36 provides that designated police stations, where suspects are usually held, should have a custody officer who will usually be the rank of sergeant. This officer is responsible for the implementation of the rights of detained persons under PACE and the Codes of Practice, and maintaining accurate custody records.

On arrival at a designated police station an arrested suspect is subject to a considerable number of rights and safeguards many of which either did not exist or were not clearly defined before PACE (See Figure 10).

Usually the first stage in this complex procedure is for the custody officer to inform or remind the suspect of the reason for the arrest. The suspect is then informed of three rights namely to have someone told of their detention, to have the services of a solicitor, and to examine the Codes of Practice. A written notice confirming all these rights is then served on the suspect. At that point the custody officer usually begins to complete the custody record and the all-important 'relevant time' is recorded. This is usually the exact time the suspect arrives at the police station although there are a number of exceptions covering instances where, for example, the suspect is arrested some distance away from the police station where he or she is wanted, or has already spent some time voluntarily attending the police station and is subsequently arrested on the spot. In the latter instance the 'relevant time' is when the arrest actually takes place and any earlier time spent at the station is not included. The entire issue of timing is crucial to the operation of PACE as will be seen later. At this stage refer to Figure 11 which depicts a custody record in abbreviated form and illustrates many of the procedures described hereon.

The right to have someone informed of the suspect's detention and to have the services of a solicitor can be delayed by up to 36 hours where a serious arrestable offence is concerned, or up to 48 hours under the Prevention of Terrorism (Temporary Provisions) Act 1989. This may only be done on the authority of a superintendent who believes that it is necessary to prevent: alerting accomplices, hinderance in the recovery of property, interference with or physical harm to others (usually witnesses), or interference with evidence. Even where access to a solicitor has been requested and agreed a superintendent may authorise the questioning of the suspect prior to the arrival of a solicitor if it is believed that delay will cause any of the factors mentioned above or immediate risk of loss or damage to property or that waiting for a solicitor would impede the progress of the investigation.

Shortly after the arrival of an arrested person at a designated police station the suspect is searched and details of all property carried on their person is recorded in the custody record. This will also include any items already seized upon the arrest of the suspect. Normally personal effects (except cash and certain valuables) and clothing are retained by the suspect, but the custody officer may seize items that could cause injury to the suspect or others, damage to property, interference with evidence, assist in the suspect's escape or may itself constitute evidence. If necessary a strip search may be conducted provided it is essential to remove an article that would have to be taken from the suspect. A strip search involves the removal of more than outer clothing and must be authorised by the custody officer. This should not be confused with intimate searches which are concerned with the examination of body orifices (except mouths) and must be authorised by at least a superintendent if there are reasonable grounds for believing that an article may be concealed which could cause physical harm to the suspect or others, or that a Class A drug (e.g. heroin, cocaine, ecstasy, morphine and LSD but not cannabis) may be concealed which was intended for others and this is the only practicable way to remove it. Intimate searches for drugs or harmful objects should be carried out by either a doctor or nurse, although in the latter instance a police officer of the same sex as the suspect may conduct the search on the authority of a superintendent. Under s117 reasonable force may be used if necessary to effect all police powers to search.

There are a number of reasons for detaining an arrested person at a police station without charge. One of the main purposes is to obtain further evidence and this is often done through interviewing the suspect. The rules governing such interviews are to be found in the Codes of Practice. In some cases a written account of the interview will be compiled containing not only what the suspect said but also where and when it took place, who were present, and all the relevant timings affecting the interview, namely its commencement and completion together with any breaks. The officer recording the interview must write all the relevant timings and sign the transcript, then give it to the suspect to read and sign or raise any disagreements regarding its contents. If it is impractical or likely to be detrimental to the interview, the investigating officer need not record the conversation until after it has taken place. However, tape-recorded interviews and video recordings are being used increasingly, particularly with regard to the more serious offences. The Codes of Practice stipulate a number of provisions designed to prevent the continuous questioning of suspects beyond certain limits. These include meal, refreshment and rest breaks that must be given and may only be delayed or interrupted if the investigating officer reasonably believes it is necessary to prevent: harm to persons or property, unnecessary further detention of the suspect, or harm to the result of the investigation.

The Codes of Practice make it clear that no police officer may obtain answers to questions by trickery or oppression and that vulnerable persons must be afforded certain safeguards. Such vulnerable persons include juveniles or the mentally ill or handicapped, in which case an 'appropriate adult' must be told of their detention and requested to attend. Juveniles must not share cells with adults or be subjected to an intimate search unless in the presence of an 'appropriate adult'. Others considered to be specially at risk include the deaf and those unable to understand English. In these circumstances a person who can use sign language or an interpreter must be present. Foreign nationals and citizens of independent Commonwealth countries must be informed as soon as possible of their right to contact their High Commission, Embassy or Consulate, or have them informed regarding the suspect's arrest and a representative must be allowed to visit the detainee. In certain instances this will be done

August 1997

Addendum

ENACTMENTS

1. The Police Act 1996 has now consolidated the relevant provisions of the Police Act 1964 and the Police and Magistrates' Courts Act 1994 mentioned on page 2.

2. On page 11 it should be noted that a new Code of Practice (A) took effect on 15 May 1997 but this only applies to police powers of stop and search. All the other Codes remain unchanged as published in the earlier document which took effect on 10 April 1995. There may be further changes during late 1997 to take account of new powers under the Knives Act 1997 (see below).

The effect of the new Code (A) is that it now provides an exception to the rule that reasonable suspicion must not be supported on the basis of personal factors alone such as a person's colour, age, hair style or manner of dress. The exception is where there is reliable information or intelligence that members of a group or gang habitually carry knives, weapons or controlled drugs unlawfully, and wear distinctive clothing or other means of identification which denote membership of it. The latter includes jewellery, insignia or tattoos. These new Codes should be borne in mind at several stages in this book, especially on pages 12 and 13.

3. Section 8 of the Knives Act 1997, when put into force, will significantly expand s60 of the Criminal Justice and Public Order Act 1994 as originally covered on pages 19 and 20 and the diagram on page 25. The effect of the Knives Act is that such authorisations may initially be given by an inspector or above (but subject to informing at least a superintendent as soon as is practicable), and that any extensions may last up to 24 hours instead of six. However, such extensions may only be authorised by a superintendent or above. Authorisations may also be given on the grounds that persons are carrying dangerous instruments or offensive weapons without good reason, but in future the grounds for making an authorisation must be stated. For a full discussion of this subject, the reader is recommended to study the article 'The Offensive Weapons Act 1996 and the Knives Act 1997 – How Effective Will They Be?' which was published in the *Justice of the Peace and Local Government Law*. Volume 161, No. 24, 14 June, 1997 and Volume 161, No. 25, 21 June, 1997. The Knives Act is due to be in force around autumn 1997.

4. Part III of the Police Act 1997 makes provision for the authorisation of the police and other law-enforcement bodies to place listening devices and cameras, etc. in premises, and to interfere with wireless telegraphy, such as blocking radio transmissions. This aspect of the Act makes it lawful for the police to enter or interfere with property or wireless telegraphy provided certain conditions are met. These include the requirement that an appropriate authorising officer must give the initial authorisation for such action.

Such persons must hold senior rank within their respective law-enforcement bodies and, as far as the police are concerned, this may not fall below the rank of commander in any of the London forces, or an assistant chief constable outside London. Such action may be taken where the authorising officer believes it necessary on the grounds that it is likely to be of substantial value in the prevention or detection of serious crime, and that it is the only way to achieve this purpose. However, except in cases of urgency, such authorisations should receive prior approval from a Commissioner where property specified in the authorisation is believed to be used wholly or mainly as a dwelling or as a bedroom in a hotel, or constitutes office premises, or if such action is likely to obtain knowledge relating to legal privilege, confidential personal information or confidential journalistic material. Authorisations issued under other procedures and any renewals should be sent for scrutiny to a Commissioner who has the power to cancel them where appropriate. An appeal may be made by an authorising officer against such decisions. A Commissioner under this part of the Act should not be confused with a police commissioner. This new body of Commis-sioners, headed by a Chief Commissioner, will be appointed under s91 of the Act and will consist of senior judges.

The nature of these provisions make them appropriate for inclusion under Chapter 3 of this book (police powers of entry and search of premises). It should be noted that this Act has not been put into force to date (1 August 1997), and that the Home Secretary shall issue a code of practice regarding Part III with the exception of the duties performed by the Commissioners appointed under s91 who will also investigate any complaints arising from the exercise of the powers under Part III. It is anticipated that these provisions will not be put into force until early 1998.

5. The Confiscation of Alcohol (Young Persons) Act 1997 should be borne in mind when reading Chapter 4 of this book, since this Act is directed towards the confiscation of alcohol under certain conditions and is therefore related to police powers of seizure. The Act provides that where persons under the age of 18 are drinking, have been drinking or are likely to be drinking alcohol in a public place, among other places (apart from licensed premises), a police officer may require them to surrender the intoxicating liquor and state their name and address. However, the person should be informed about the police officer's suspicion beforehand and warned that failure to surrender the drink and give his name and address could result in his arrest. Failure to comply will render the person liable to arrest without warrant unless they have reasonable excuse. If the alcohol is surrendered, the police may dispose of it in any way they consider appropriate. It should be noted that no power of search is conferred upon the police in order to find intoxicating liquor. The provisions of this Act also apply to 18 year olds and over who may be supplying drink to those below this age. This statute came into force on 1 August 1997.

6. Further arrestable offences under s24 of PACE have been created by virtue of the Protection from Harassment Act 1997. This Act is intended to deal with those who cause harassment (which includes 'stalkers'), and those who put people in fear of violence. The offence of harassment attracts a maximum prison sentence of six months but the 1997 Act specifically makes this an arrestable offence, and therefore it should be included in the list after ticket and taxi

touting on pages 41 and 49. Since this is a summary only offence, like ticket and taxi touting, it may be excluded from other arrestable offences that may be attempted. When a person is convicted of the offence of harassment the court may also impose a restraining order upon the offender, which prohibits conduct likely to continue causing the victim distress. If the offender breaches such an order this will constitute an offence leading to a maximum of five years' imprisonment, and therefore this automatically falls under the heading of an arrestable offence.

A conviction for the offence of putting people in fear of violence can also lead to a maximum five-year prison term and is subsequently arrestable; this also applies to a breach of a restraining order that may also be imposed on a conviction for this offence. Finally, this Act contains civil remedies against harassment including the provision that where an injunction is imposed to prevent further distress to the victim and the defendant breaches its conditions, this too can result in a maximum five-year custodial sentence, thereby automatically making it an arrestable offence. With the exception of the criminal sanctions applicable to the breaching of civil injunctions, the provisions of this Act came into force on 16 June 1997. The remainder is likely to become effective around autumn 1997.

ERRATA

References on pages 42 and 49 to 'buggery with a boy under 16 or with anyone who did not consent' should be amended to read 'buggery with a person under 16'.

The centre of the diagram on page 49 which depicts how arrestable offences can be transformed into serious arrestable offences should also contain the following: 'any person's death or serious injury'. This is confirmed on page 43.

Leonard Jason-Lloyd
1 August 1997

automatically by the police although if the suspect is seeking political asylum or is a political refugee then this will not be done unless the detainee specifically requests it.

Intoxicated and generally incoherent persons must not be interviewed but medical assistance should be sought instead. However, these provisions may be waived on the authority of a superintendent if an immediate risk of harm to persons or property is likely to occur if an interview is not conducted immediately.

As stated earlier, there are strict time limits on the detention of persons without charge. In most cases an arrested person may not be detained without charge for more than 24 hours after the commencement of the relevant time unless a serious arrestable offence has been committed. If the latter applies a superintendent may extend this to 36 hours if there are reasonable grounds to believe that it is necessary to secure or preserve evidence or that evidence may be obtained by further questioning.

However, the authorising officer must be satisfied that the investigation is proceeding efficiently. (The initial maximum period of police detention without charge under the Prevention of Terrorism [Temporary Provisions] Act 1989 is 48 hours which can be extended). Where a serious arrestable offence has been committed and it is necessary to keep a suspect more than 36 hours, the police may bring the suspect before a magistrates' court in order to extend the time limit by up to a maximum of a further 60 hours. Where these offences are concerned, 96 hours is therefore the absolute maximum that the police may detain a suspect without charge provided the magistrates are satisfied that the police are conducting the investigation efficiently and that it is necessary to secure or preserve evidence or that evidence may be obtained by further questioning. Such hearings before magistrates are not public and the suspect must be legally represented if requested. A further safeguard under PACE regarding the detention of suspects is the provision for periodic reviews of each person whether or not they have been charged. If they have not been charged the review officer must be at least the rank of inspector and should conduct the first review not later than six hours after the time the suspect's detention was first authorised. The review officer must subsequently make any further reviews at intervals of nine hours. Where a suspect has been charged it is the custody officer who is responsible for making reviews although this procedure is rarely necessary since suspects are usually brought before the court at the earliest opportunity once charged.

There are a number of courses of action open to the police when either their investigations have been completed or the detention time expires. If the custody officer, having consulted with the investigating officer, decides at the end of the investigation that there is sufficient evidence and the suspect is charged, he will then either be released on conditional or unconditional bail to appear at a later date before a magistrates' court; kept in police custody until the next available court sitting if his name and address are unknown or doubted, or it is believed necessary for his or others' personal protection or their property, or it is believed he will abscond or interfere with the investigation or generally obstruct the course of justice. The suspect may also be dealt with in two further ways depending upon the offence and surrounding circumstances. The first is by reporting (but not charging) the suspect for the offence and then proceeding by way of a summons. The second is by giving the suspect a caution. The latter is used where the offence is not particularly serious and the suspect does not have a previous record.

If the suspect has not been charged and the detention time has expired or is close to expiry, the police will either have to release him outright or, if they feel that more evidence may come to light later, they can release the suspect on unconditional bail. This means he will have to attend the police station at a later date and could be detained without charge again on the return visit if the police reasonably believe that it is necessary in order to secure or preserve evidence or obtain evidence by questioning him. However, the second detention may only take place if there is any unused time from the first occasion. The suspect's obligation to return can be cancelled by the custody officer in writing where appropriate although he can be re-arrested if further evidence comes to light. In such cases the detention time starts afresh.

The power for the police to impose conditional bail where necessary in respect of charged suspects has been introduced by the Criminal Justice and Public Order Act 1994. This means that the police have powers almost identical to the courts with regard to restricting a person's liberty while out on bail. These conditions include prohibiting a released suspect on bail from going near certain people or places, imposing a curfew, and requiring the suspect to report to the police station on a daily basis. Unlike the courts, however, the police do not have the power to require that a person resides at a bail hostel.

Proposed law reform regarding police evidence is soon due to be enacted.* Under the current Criminal Procedure and Investigations Bill, the Home Secretary

---

* This Bill received the Royal Assent on 4th July 1996.

will be under a duty to formulate Codes of Practice regarding police evidence. This will place them under a greater obligation to record and preserve all evidence in a criminal investigation and also make this available for inspection where appropriate.

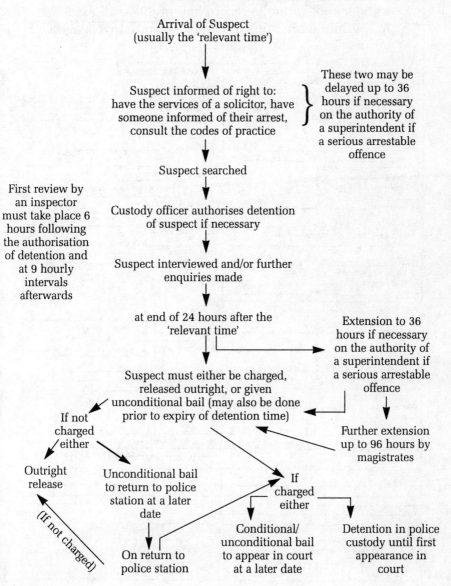

FIGURE 10

POLICE DETENTION – THE BASIC RULES

Arrival of Suspect
(usually the 'relevant time')

Suspect informed of right to:
have the services of a solicitor, have
someone informed of their arrest,
consult the codes of practice

These two may be
delayed up to 36
hours if necessary
on the authority of
a superintendent if
a serious arrestable
offence

Suspect searched

First review by
an inspector
must take place 6
hours following
the authorisation
of detention and
at 9 hourly
intervals
afterwards

Custody officer authorises detention
of suspect if necessary

Suspect interviewed and/or further
enquiries made

at end of 24 hours after the
'relevant time'

Extension to 36
hours if necessary
on the authority of
a superintendent if
a serious arrestable
offence

Suspect must either be charged,
released outright, or given
unconditional bail (may also be done
prior to expiry of detention time)

Further extension
up to 96 hours by
magistrates

If not
charged
either

Outright
release

Unconditional bail
to return to police
station at a later
date

If
charged
either

(If not charged)

On return to
police station

Conditional/
unconditional bail
to appear in court
at a later date

Detention in police
custody until first
appearance in
court

FIGURE 11

CUSTODY RECORD

BARCHESTER POLICE

POLICE STATION:	CUSTODY NO.

REASON FOR ARREST:	CONDITION ON ARRIVAL AT POLICE STATION:

A notice of my rights has been read to me and I have also been provided with a written notice.

Signature of person detained: _____

Time: _____ Date: _____

Signature of appropriate
adult/interpreter: _____
Time _____ Date: _____

Notification of detention to named person
requested/not requested

Named Person: _____

Time: _____ Date: _____

"I want a solicitor as soon as practicable"
Signature: _____

Time: _____ Date: _____
Signature of appropriate
adult/interpreter: _____
Time: _____ Date: _____

"I do not want a solicitor at this time"

Signature: _____

Time: _____ Date: _____
Signature of appropriate
adult/interpreter: _____
Time: _____ Date: _____

CUSTODY OFFICER:
Signature: _____
Name, Rank & No: _____

REASON FOR DETENTION:

Surname:
(Mr. Mrs. Miss) _____

First Names: _____
_____

Address: _____
_____
_____
_____

Occupation: _____

Age: _____ D.o.B. __/__/__
Place of Birth: _____
Ident. Code: _____ Height: _____ Sex: M/F

Arrested by:
Name: _____
[block capitals]
Rank: _____ No: _____ Station: _____
Arrested at:[place] _____

	Time	Date
Arrested at		
Arrival at station		

PROPERTY [FOUND ON PERSON OR ELSEWHERE]

	YES	NO	RETAINED BY POLICE REASON
1. CASH £			
2.			
3.			
4.			
5.			

SIGNATURE OF PRISONER AGREEING WITH ABOVE, [Any refusal to sign should be recorded]

Rank, No., of Officer searching: _____ Signature: _____

60

FIGURE 11 (cont.)

RELEVANT TIME	DATE	TIME		REVIEW OF DETENTION DUE AT		
				1st	2nd	3rd
				4th	5th	6th

Date	Time	Details of any action/occurrence involving the detained person

7

Abuse of Police Powers

The ever-increasing complexities and hazards that form part of the daily life of the average police officer must inevitably lead to occasional mishaps. Errors of judgement such as excessive force used in moments of stress are easily understood by those regularly confronted with the rigours of operational policing but many of those not possessing such insight find it difficult to understand. However, there are occasions when certain police actions give rise to legitimate concern and these must be addressed in order to maintain public confidence.

The abuse of police powers can take a number of forms. First, there are transgressions against the Codes of Practice. Although breaches of the Codes do not themselves constitute crimes or civil wrongs, the courts may include evidence of a breach as part of other proceedings. The main effect of the Codes of Practice is on internal disciplinary measures taken within the police service whenever a breach occurs and this is the direction that most complaints of this nature follow.

Secondly, there are a range of civil wrongs and even criminal acts that can be committed by the police under a variety of circumstances. Some of the most common are assault, false imprisonment and criminal damage. Assaults are the most prevalent source of the more serious complaints against the police. By the very nature of increased violence in society, the police themselves bear the brunt of much of this disturbing trend. This is borne out by the dramatic rise in the number of assaults on police in recent years. However, any force used by the police must be reasonable in the circumstances and anything in excess of this can constitute both a criminal act and a civil wrong. Criminal proceedings against the police can be extremely difficult to initiate since many cases will often contain special defences if the police were acting within their powers. It is therefore usual to take civil action where the remedy sought will be damages. Assaults can take many forms and need not involve serious injury or any injury at all since any direct, intentional and unlawful application of physical force constitutes an assault. If the force used was reasonable and necessary in the circumstances and within the powers held by the police it will not give rise to successful civil action. The courts, however, take full account of the circumstances confronting the police especially when they use force in self-defence. In *Palmer-v.-Regina (1971)* Lord Morris of Borth-Y-Gest said that when a person is violently attacked and it is necessary to act in self defence, they cannot be expected to measure the exact degree of force necessary when in a state of anguish.

False imprisonment is the correct legal term for what is commonly known as wrongful arrest. If a person experiences any unlawful restriction on their liberty this amounts to false imprisonment and need not only involve being locked-up or confined within an enclosed space. Therefore if a person is unlawfully arrested or subjected to an unlawful stop and search for instance, even though this may have taken place in the open, the mere fact that they were not at liberty to move as they wished constitutes false imprisonment. Physical contact need not take place either since even words or conduct which will lead the victim to believe that they are not at liberty to move freely can be sufficient to prove false imprisonment if the restriction was unlawful. The duration of an unlawful constraint on a citizen's liberty does not necessarily have to be long. Although the damages will usually be commensurate with the length of time, other factors such as the location of the restraint and the likelihood of embarrassment will also be taken into account. An example of this would occur, for instance, where the victim was searched or arrested in the street in full view of passers-by.

Criminal damage can occur in many forms but some of those attributable to the police are instances where property is damaged in the course of entering and searching premises or where property is damaged in the course of an arrest. Criminal damage is a criminal offence but for reasons already outlined it is more usual for civil action to be taken in this respect. The civil actions relevant to this offence are trespass to goods or negligence. However, the latter is easier to prove and generally more appropriate since the plaintiff has to prove in the former instance that the damage was deliberate whereas an action in negligence requires evidence of insufficient care rather than wilful damage.

It must be stressed that if the police can prove they had lawful reasons for their actions and exercised these powers in a reasonable manner, then no legal action can be taken against them. However, transgressions against the Codes of Practice and other forms of police misconduct which in themselves do not give rise to legal action can be dealt with through the official police complaints procedure that was instituted through PACE, although a number of prosecutions have arisen as a result of this procedure being used initially. PACE also instituted the independent Police Complaints Authority replacing the Police Complaints Board as the body responsible for investigating serious complaints against the police.

Complaints against the police may be initiated in several ways (See *Figure 12*). The complainant may make the allegation personally either by visiting the police station or in writing to the chief constable or commissioner, whichever applies. Alternatively, the complaint may be directed to any of the above through another party acting on the complainant's behalf such as a legal adviser or a friend. The vast majority of complaints are not serious and are usually dealt with at an informal level. This will include, for instance, an apology where the officer was unjustly rude to the complainant, or by an explanation if, for example, the officer appeared to be rude but was acting in an emergency. This procedure is known as an informal resolution.

If the nature of the complaint appears to be serious either by inferring a more serious breach of police discipline or even legally actionable offences, the matter will be placed into the hands of a senior police officer who will investigate the allegations. On the completion of the investigation the senior police officer will then report his or her findings to both the head of their respective police force and the Police Complaints Authority. If the allegation is proven and confined solely to a breach of internal discipline, the officer may be subjected to any number of internal sanctions via a police disciplinary hearing which can be modified either way by the Police Complaints Authority. These include reprimands, internal fines, demotion or dismissal.

Complaints involving serious criminal allegations are investigated under the direct supervision of the Police Complaints Authority. Once this has been completed either the chief officer of the relevant police force or the Police Complaints Authority may decide to refer the case to the Director of Public Prosecutions for consideration to prosecute the officer.

In addition to complaints against police officers arising from specific incidents, there is also scope for the public to complain about general police policy. This can take a variety of forms depending upon the nature of the complaint. If, for instance, a citizen wishes to complain about the lack of police patrols in a particular street or neighbourhood their grievance will be best directed to the officer in charge of their local police division (usually a superintendent). Should the complaint be of a more widespread or general nature the grievance should be directed to the chief constable or, if in London, the commissioner. Any dissatisfaction with the response could be addressed to a number of sources including local councillors, constituency MPs or even pressure groups or the press.

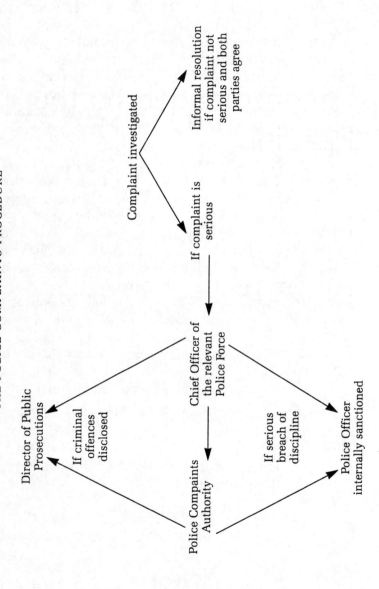

FIGURE 12

THE POLICE COMPLAINTS PROCEDURE

Complaint investigated

Informal resolution if complaint not serious and both parties agree

If complaint is serious

Chief Officer of the relevant Police Force

Director of Public Prosecutions

If criminal offences disclosed

Police Compaints Authority

If serious breach of discipline

Police Officer internally sanctioned

Recommended Further Reading

H. Levenson, F. Fairweather and E. Cape. *Police Powers – A Practitioner's Guide* 3rd Edition (The Legal Action Group, 1996).

K. Lidstone and Palmer. *Bevan and Lidstone's: The Investigation of Crime – A Guide to Police Powers* 2nd Edition (Butterworths, 1996).

M. Zander. *The Police and Criminal Evidence Act 1984.* 3rd Edition (Sweet & Maxwell, 1995).

J. Harrison and S. Cragg. *Police Misconduct: Legal Remedies.* 3rd Edition (The Legal Action Group, 1995)

J. English and R. Card. *Butterworths Police Law.* 4th Edition (Butterworths, 1994).

L. Jason-Lloyd. *The Criminal Justice and Public Order Act 1994. – A Basic Guide for Practitioners* (Frank Cass, 1996).

Glossary

CIVIL WRONGS (OR TORTS)

The law of Tort covers a variety of civil wrongs but for the purposes of police powers the main areas we should concern ourselves with are negligence, trespass to land, goods or to the person. Torts often overlap with other areas of law, particularly criminal law, such as assaults for instance. In such cases the victim may be able to obtain both the punishment of the offender in the criminal courts, and redress in the civil courts by suing for unliquidated damages. In the latter instance the person bringing the action is called the Plaintiff and the civil action involved is the Tort of trespass to the person. Since the law of Tort comes under the heading of civil (or private) law, cases of this kind are tried in civil courts where proceedings are often very different compared to the criminal courts.

THE COMMON LAW

The most important source of law in England is that made by Parliament in the form of Statute or Act of Parliament.

However, it is impossible for Parliament to legislate on every issue of human activity and inevitably there are gaps in the law. It is the common law that fills in the gaps left by Statute and consists of judgments made in the courts based on precedent (decisions on earlier cases being applied to later cases that are sufficiently similar). The common law is therefore made by the judges but it can be overridden by Statute.

DIRECTOR OF PUBLIC PROSECUTIONS (DPP)

The DPP is a senior civil servant appointed by the Home Secretary who may either be a barrister or solicitor of at least ten years' standing. Apart from overall responsibility for the Crown Prosecution Service which conducts most criminal proceedings on behalf of the police, the DPP is also expected to conduct cases of a difficult or important nature, and take decisions in cases involving offences only she can prosecute (e.g., the offence of riot). The DPP is directly responsible to the Attorney-General.

JUVENILE

Any person under the age of 18 years before the courts is regarded as a juvenile, although for general police purposes a juvenile is regarded as an under 17 year old. Under the present criminal justice system 10 to 17 year olds inclusive may be tried for offences usually before the youth court (formerly known as juvenile courts).

REASONABLE FORCE

This term is important in the exercise of many police

powers since the police often find themselves faced with situations where tact and reason fail, and force has to be used as a last resort. It is the general rule that such force must be reasonable in all the circumstances although it is impossible to codify the degree necessary to fit individual circumstances. Many factors have to be considered when assessing whether the force used was reasonable. This will include surrounding circumstances, the perceived state of mind of the accused, the evil that was being prevented, and many more.

RECORDABLE OFFENCES

These are offences which, when proven, must be recorded in national police records and the fingerprints of the convicted person must be taken accordingly. Any offence which is punishable by imprisonment or is one of several specified offences (such as tampering with a motor vehicle, and loitering or soliciting for the purposes of prostitution), falls under the heading of a recordable offence.

SUMMARY OFFENCES

These are the less serious crimes that Statute stipulates are triable only in the magistrates' courts. This covers dozens of offences many of which are non-arrestable and include nearly all motoring offences.

Index

Table of Statutes

Table of Cases